HOW TO
GUIDE THE
APPRENTICE

HOW TO GUIDE THE APPRENTICE

Temple Garden Tattoo:
The Professional Standard

JD Julian

Library of Congress Control Number: 2012906773
ISBN: Hardcover   978-1-4691-2535-0
               Softcover   978-1-4691-2534-3
               Ebook   978-1-4691-2536-7

This book was printed in the United States of America.

To order additional copies of this book, contact:
Xlibris Corporation
1-888-795-4274
www.Xlibris.com
Orders@Xlibris.com
112122

CONTENTS

DEDICATION

A special thanks to my friends and family, my Grandparent's, my wife Shayla, and especially my three kiddo's Jacob, Sara and Kaitlin. Each and every one of you, and I mean all of you, have in some way given me the drive and determination it took to complete my dreams. I hope to make you proud.

Thank you Shanty Jinkins of Texas Inkslingers in Dumas Texas for the opportunity to complete my apprenticeship, and gain exposure.

INTRODUCTION

Like most ancient manuscripts' of its nature. Tattooing is a sacred craft that has been passed down from generation to generation, and performed by a highly regarded member of their society. This book will not teach you how to tattoo. This book will help implement a structured curriculum for all, apprentice.

ABOUT THE AUTHOR

JD Julian

By Shayla Funk

Now JD was born in Utah raised in Colorado and found his home here in Texas. He has an extensive background in the human body. He was a personal trainer and physical therapy tech for many years before deciding to become a tattoo artist. I will never forget the day he decided he wanted to be an artist. Shortly after his second child was born we decided to go get tattoos to commemorate this wonderful event. Well needless to say the tattoos did not come out so great so we decided to go back to the shop we had them done at to speak with the owner. I had no idea what was fixing to happen, JD explained the disappointment in the tattoos to the owner and as any decent business man would do the owner asked what he could do to make this right. What came next I would have never guessed in a million years, JD asked for the opportunity to be an apprentice at this shop so he could make sure this didn't happen to anyone else, and that is where the tattoo journey began. For those of you who have not had the honor of meeting my husband I encourage you to take a trip to Temple Garden Tattoo and take a seat in his chair. I have seen this man through the darkest times and greatest triumphs and he always finds a way to bring his dreams to life. I cannot tell you how many times he has been told no or just brushed off as if he didn't matter. Regardless of everyone else's beliefs he literally took himself from nothing and found a way to make his love of art his life.

CHAPTER ONE
Basic Outline of Apprenticeship

1. What is expected
2. Daily shop duties
3. Shop assignments
4. Sterilization

What is Expected

This book will guide the apprentice through the basic standards of this industry. Every apprenticeship will differ, so follow all instructions of your Master closely.

      I.   How long should the apprenticeship be
     II.   Terms of contract
    III.   Apprentice terminology

As an apprentice, I saw how many people come through the doors asking for an apprenticeship if you are one of the lucky few who have been chosen, congratulations. It's a long road ahead, keep your head down, and absorb as much as possible . . .

How long should the apprenticeship be

All tattoo apprenticeships are different, but to answer the question. The average apprenticeship takes 2-6 years and the cost may vary depending on curriculum and extent of apprenticeship.

2year Apprenticeships:

> Consist of basic shop knowledge of daily shop duties, application of cross contamination, complete basic apprenticeship curriculum requirements, minimum of 1500hours of instruction and performance. How to, properly perform all procedures.

4year Apprenticeships:

> This takes the basic skills of the apprentice and develops their abilities into a tattoo artist. This apprentice has paid their shop

dues and has a basic knowledge of their own equipment. This is when you as an apprentice obtain your first shop equipment, minimum of an additional 750hours of instruction and performance of curriculum.

6year Apprenticeships:

Taking the necessary steps toward becoming a, Journeyman tattooist. They still work under the watchful eye and guidance of their Master. This stage of your career is when you start to see a small commission, to help further your Journeyman status. The Master you study under will determine your placement in the shop.

Terms of contract:

Normal terms of contracts are basic and follow a strict guideline. If you feel like a contract is too long, or is a bit one sided, make sure to get a clear overview of your expectations and what is being offered in return. Knowing what you got yourself into is really important. Be prepared for unreasonable signatures, date and Notarize . . .

Make sure you keep and fulfill your end of the contract at all cost. If you half-ass this, you will probably half-ass your tattoo career. Keep in mind that even the great struggled, if you're not cut out for this line of work best to find out now and not six months into an apprenticeship.

Contracts may also consist of a non-compete clause, which would prevent the apprentice from working in or opening their own shop within a radius of an area and terms of years of competition. Never sign a contract if you're not in complete agreement to the terms, or not prepared to agree to terms that are not clear. Tattoo apprenticeships are not for just anyone.

Any person seeking a tattoo apprenticeship could be required to provide documentation of satisfactory completion of a minimum of 5 hours of health education to include but not limited to; Blood borne disease, sterilization and antiseptic techniques related to tattooing, first aid and CPR.

As the apprentice, your patience is a virtue that will be tested. Not only that but not all apprenticeships are paid positions. This is what apprenticeships are all about, an unpaid internship with a slight chance of ever making it as an artist.

Apprentice terminology:

Anatomy: the science dealing with the structure of animals and plants

Antiseptic: free form or cleaned of germs and other microorganisms

Apprentice: a person who works for another in order to learn a trade

Art: a field, genre, or category of art

Booth: a stall, or light structure for the sale of goods, as at the market

Client: a customer or patron

Concepts: an idea of something formed by mentally combining all its characteristics

Contract: an agreement enforceable by law

Design: to make drawings, preliminary sketches, or plans

Epidermis: the outer, nonvascular, non-sensitive layer of the skin, covering the dermis.

Fungi: single-celled or multinucleate organisms

Germicidal soap: hospital grade microorganism cleaner

Instruments: a mechanical tool or instrument, especially one used for delicate or precision work

Lead artist: the most experienced tattoo artist, the shop Manager

License holder: a person 18 years or older who owns, operates, or maintains a tattoo studio

Machine: a device that transmits or modifies force or motion

Master: a person eminently skilled in something, as an occupation, art, or science

Portfolio: a flat, portable case for carrying loose papers, drawings, etc.

Prep work: preparation or light work

Sanitation: the development and application of sanitary measures for the sake of protecting health

Sharps: bio-hazardous materials or needled points, or scalpel otherwise penetrating the skin

Single use: one-time use, one person use only

Sketch book: practice, doodle, or concept design pad of paper

Sterilization: the destruction of living microorganisms, as pathogenic or bacteria and spores

Tattoo studio: a permanent non-dwelling building in accordance with applicable zoning codes where tattoos are performed

Universal precautions: a method of infection control in which treat all blood borne pathogens and body fluids and taking proper precautions.

Apprentice terminology:

Department: Department of State Health Services

Germicidal solution: an agent that kills microorganisms on hard surfaces

Aftercare instructions: written and oral instructions given to every client, specific to procedures

Invasive: entry through the skin by insertion or incision

A.S.T.M.: American Society for Testing Materials

Restricted: use of all measures to prevent unauthorized entry

Point of origin: an area where the biomedical waste is generated

Public sharps collection program: a service to assist a safe disposal of material

Treatment: any process that includes steam, chemical, to render noninfectious by sterilization

Agent: an inspector from the State Department of Health

Transfer: movement of bio-waste within a tattoo studio

Biological hazard symbol: a universal symbol used as a warning against the threat of living organisms

Daily Shop Duties

All shops have daily, weekly, bi-weekly, monthly, quarterly, and yearly duties that must be done. By knowing your duties, and creating a checklist, will improve your skills as an apprentice.

Basic Daily duties

Opening:

> The shop needs wiped down from top to bottom, all glass is to be cleaned, all art prepped for presentation, all stations must be stocked and ready for the day, the bathroom must be spotless, now is a great time to sweep and mop. All opening procedures must be completed before the shop doors open for business. Spot mop here and there as needed throughout the day, especially if you are one of the messy ones.

Closing:

> Shop needs a compete tear-down of stations, sanitize, sweep and clean up, trashes must be taken out and all equipment, utensils, or instruments must go through a sterilization cycle. Everything is set-up and ready for the next day. Sweep, mop and take out trash.

> Now these are the basic everyday open-close task's, and just because I didn't list it, doesn't excuse you from doing the work. As the apprentice there is a chain of command you must follow if you feel disrespected as the low-man, before you allow it to eat you up inside. Reflect back on who you are and what you are doing.

As an apprentice grows and finds their niche, all tasks will come as second nature. Once daily tasks are routine and at the standards of the Master; the task list will grow from sweeping and mopping, from breaking down a tattoo booth, into sanitation and sterilization, then basic art designs and finally the chance to set-up the tattoo booth. After all the checklist have been completed and before any opportunity to advance to the next level then before you know it, you'll be doing your first tattoo.

Develop the daily duty log sheets in the following categories:

Opening shop

>   Gallery
>   Tattoo booth
>   Sterilization station
>   Art desk/Office
>   Restroom

Closing shop

>   Sweep and Mop
>   Sterilization station
>   Restock
>   All shop trash

Daily task

>   Practice art book
>   Daily required curriculum
>   Sanitation and sterilization
>   Shop daily tasks

No apprentice will have it easy. This guide just makes it a bit easier and keeps a consistent curriculum for all apprenticeships.

Although every task gets repetitive a good apprentice will fly through the curriculum with no hang ups, as long as you keep progressing and have not been reprimanded for performance, your apprenticeship should stay in good standing.

Practice Tattoo Sketch Book is a great form of assignments for any apprentice. Being an Artist is our goal, and practice is our life, but inspiration is not always at our top hand.

Do not believe every time we touch something it will turn into a masterpiece. If you are good at art it will not be necessarily true that you will be a good tattooist. If you want to master both follow the instruction of your Master, find out what helps your hand strength. There is nothing worse than a tattoo that wasn't applied correctly or a tattooist taking credit for the tattoo they do before they know whose machine they hold in their hand, or the artist whom designed that tattoo.

If working hard for no pay and putting everything you earn for the next 6 years back into what you need to get to the next level, the Tattoo Gods will find you a place to build your name as a Tattoo Artist.

Art—Sketchbooks—Binders & Portfolios—these are just a start of an apprenticeship, and by far one of the most important elements to the trade. If anyone asked me what it takes to be a tattoo artist my answer would be, show me your portfolio, what type of medium do they use and then what type of machines do they use? By the end of those questions I have my answer. But there are a few that get the chance to come into my booth and the next 15 minutes are critical. The Personal hygiene—knowledge—personality—all around, how well I like you in my shop.

Now all that's expected of an apprentice is to know how to properly clean. Some basic terminology, what types of equipment and instruments that are being used and how to apply all aspects of the tattoo. The art portfolio helps the apprentice show their style and technique. Most tattoo artist will not take on an apprentice if they have hardly any knowledge of the tattoo process or what they are going to be doing to the body.

Like most of my peers we share some kind of medical or science background. To be a tattoo artist is to be a topical surgeon, so just to pick up a tool and use it a couple of times does not entitle you to be a tattoo artist. It takes years of study to master the necessary skills of a tattoo artist.

- Thousands of hours of curriculum
- Hundreds of documented tattoo's
- Years of study

That's just the curriculum of the apprentice. Not including all the non-documented practice work you get and if your apprenticeship is anything like mine, a lot of your practice will be on yourself. My thighs and calves were my practice work before I was allowed to tattoo clients. The Master will determine when you get the chance to advance.

It seems to be more and more geeks off the street trying to do their thing. That's not the most ideal way to start. If you like that geek-out look, a twitchy lil beady eyed fool and we all know the type. Be careful on how you choose the apprentice you have servicing your shop. It helps to have some kind of prior relationship with the person you trust to educate in this field of: Body-mod, dermal-implants, scarification, tongue splitting, piercings, and tattooing.

One of the hardest temptations for an apprentice is for someone to offer the apprentice the opportunity to tattoo them, if you have any pride in what you are becoming. Do not do anything that might jeopardize the chances of a realized dream. This is what differ the paid tattoo artist, from all others with just a tool in their hand. So think before you ink, otherwise you will stink.

Shop Assignments

Each apprentice should have a skill that sets them apart from all others in that shop. This is probably why you have been chosen to be an apprentice. Each assignment will be designed to build weakness and gain prospective. Not every tattoo will be done your way, or they style you prefer to tattoo best. It took me six years before I started getting any request for my artwork, and in those six years I kept true to my style. With practice I developed my hand and worked on my skills. Now I can draw with confidence.

As any good apprentice you should have some kind of sketch-pad, art book, or canvas. These materials are an important part of the development of the apprentice, without them you will never reach your goal. So if you fall short of your ability to draw, or any art assignments fall short of your Masters standards of tattoo art designs, then I suggest taking a course in art basics or any continuing education from your community college, for basic structure or inspiration and guidance.

Shop assignments are structured to develop your skills as an artist and better your performance as a tattoo artist. The things you practice, develops your hand and gives you a good idea of what you're good at. Now let's go on to test the waters and draw some basic tattoo designs.

Art Assignment:

basic tattoo designs

25—crosses
25—hearts
25—wings

24

Once you get all basic tattoo designs completed, get a few useable designs. With the final designs you have chosen, put all three designs together to make a tattoo concept. Concept designs are a great way to build a portfolio.

basic tattoo concepts

> 15—Feminine
> 15—Masculine
> 15—Both

Now that all designs are finalized, and concepts are complete. Fine-line all your work you feel is tattoo worthy get the approval from your Instructor before your art work is complete. All designs are to go in a shop binder or file cabinet, make sure to label, sign and date all your artwork. Concepts are to be finalized; fine line work, black and grey, color and any style you do well should be showcased in your art portfolio, as the first opportunity to publicly display your art work.

Assignments are not all about drawing or painting, by opening up your artistic views you can gain prospective and find inspiration. Take out your camera with the right light a perfect setting you might just capture a masterpiece. Now by taking comparison shots of your subject with multiple cameras capture the clear natural nature of your subject. Develop the photos in any style format you prefer, after the photos have been chosen for your photo portfolio present your best interpretation of what you see for your art portfolio.

Take your time, this might take more than one try to get the desired look, or effect like depth or contrast. No art work is bad art work, that's just the bitter taste of the critic's pallet. Never let it get you down, only 1/3 of your public will like your work. Practice your style and learn technique to improve your apprenticeship portfolio.

Not all shop assignments are art related, there is filing and documenting that must be done, on top of any locally bought items that must be on the too do list. The maintenance of the shop is one of the apprentices' duties. Make sure all studio and out-door lights are working properly, keep up the parking-lot, if any repairs are necessary make sure you have the approval of the Master or license holders permission. As the apprentice you will understand doing the job right the first time is the only way of a true Master.

Shop assignments are designed to take you out of your element. The skills you learn and take with you along the way will give you a greater prospective on the art work of other tattoo artist. Take the skills you need to improve the style of tattoos you will give and stay consistent.

By taking the time to study past tattoo artist you will learn the history of where your profession started and why. Those who came before us have much to teach, and hardly any curriculum material printed. So we do our best to learn by instruction of students of masters. No matter what generation of tattoo artist you are, hold a consistent curriculum in order to successfully pass on our knowledge.

Not all tattoo artists are reputable, but not all tattoo artists are of criminal influence either. Only a slight percentage of artists are of this nature. Most of the tattoo artist today are Professionals and hold a high standard of professionalism in their studios.

Take pride in any assignment that you've been instructed or commissioned for. You never know when a door will open up, and success comes pouring in. If your work is appreciated, you will gain favor in a shop or even better recognition as a flash artist and become published.

Now after a few basic designs have been worked to the final line-work, take on the challenge of creating a sleeve concept. Look at the structure or build of the arm, follow the contours of the arm and make the designs flow with the body. It makes for a better sleeve, if it is not too cluttered.

In the world of tattoos, there is nothing better than an opportunity to design a sleeve concept. This can separate the artist from the tattooist. No matter your style, this is the opportunity to showcase your work of living art. If the designs are too small for the concept, the sleeve will appear over worked and unplanned. Try to keep your sessions at 4 hours. The human body is amazing but the body can only handle so much trauma, before calling it quits.

design a sleeve concept

The sleeve concept must be clear and distinct designs these are the largest billboards available for an artist. Design the sleeve from top of the deltoid, down to the forearm and stop your design about 6 inches from the wrist unless instructed otherwise.

Design the concept with the following:

- Three types of flowers
- Revolver pistol with scroll work and an engraving "Lady"
- Pair of birds
- Use two of any elements, to fill in space. Earth, Wind, Fire, Water.

Complete the full sleeve design, for presentation.

The Master will test the apprentice in all attributes of curriculum, and the apprentice should be expected to produce tattoo designs, and tattoo concepts as a weekly routine. Quarterly the apprentice must present all art assignments, designs and concepts in a complete format ready to present in a portfolio.

As the apprentice gains experience they should become responsible for creating original art work on their own. The Master sets the guidelines and all deadlines. Complete all tasks promptly and to the best of your ability, remember a client might not like the design on first, second, or even the third presentation. Having a face to face design consultation will cut down any miss communication of the tattoo concept being commissioned, and offers a personal touch of T.L.C. to an already nervous client.

The Apprentice must learn the value of the education, well-before the opportunity to price the cost of a tattoo. The Master sets the cost of all tattoos for the shop and the apprentice, to overstep any boundary as the apprentice is a punishable offense and treated accordingly.

STERILIZATION

Sanitation is basic knowledge of the apprenticeship. Most bacteria live on our hair follicles and the cross sections layers of skin, that's just the start of the many surfaces in a studio. Before the tattoo, is ever set, knowledge of universal health precautions, health code procedures, O.S.H.A. and H.I.P.A.A., and all bio-waste disposal, is required by the State Department of Health.

Knowledge of cross contamination is the most important factor in keeping a safe clean tattoo studio. By keeping the tattoo booth clean and tidy, will insure that all equipment is in its place and ready for use.

The knowledge of, all micro-organisms, aerobic, anaerobic bacteria and the many viruses that you are responsible for knowing how to identify and universal precautions that must be used during all tattoo procedures.

The epidermis is the outer most layer of skin that protects the body from injury or parasites. It is a working organism so a touch of compassion and sensitivity would be nice. The proper tattoo is set in the depths of the epidermis layer, just above the dermis layer of skin. The dermis layer of skin is quite sensitive and susceptible to infection, the dermis layer of skin houses anaerobic bacteria and viruses.

By popping on a hardy pair of gloves, every step of the tattooing process will protect you and your clients from many forms of bacteria, viruses, and fungi. By knowing how to identify aerobic bacteria, viruses, any forms of fungi, and understanding how to use the proper universal precautions. Protect yourself from body fluids and microorganisms by gloving up, and follow any cross contamination procedures. You will need a pair of gloves for the following procedures:

- cleaning station: all stations must be cleaned and sanitized
- set up prep: needle configurations, tubes, prep of equipment
- client prep: clean, shave, prep and place stencil
- tattoo: at every starting point of the tattoo
- after care: clean tattoo, place bandage, and explain care
- tear down: disposal of bio-materials and the cleanup of the station
- sterilization: the prep cleaning, scrubbing, package, sterilize

Cross contamination is a basic knowledge of what you touch has now become dirty. Keep all the equipment you use on a daily basis protected with the proper protective covering. Keep it basic and find a routine that fits you. By protecting all your equipment and any instruments used during all procedures will cut down on microorganism transfer, and spore growth.

Watch what you touch and wash your hands after taking off each pair of gloves, before entering or leaving a tattoo station. Only when the apprentice can successfully pass off state health code practices and universal precaution as a second nature, will an apprentice find advancement.

As the apprentice you will learn proper log sheets for daily sterilization, weekly maintenance, and cleaning, and monthly spore test. Keep all the records of use, cleaning, and spore test.

If you're not sure how to prep for the sterilization process, make sure to follow the Masters strict instructions:

- properly allow instruments to soak
- run ultrasonic cycle
- glove up rinse and clean instruments
- allow to dry, seal, sign, date, log sterile pouches
- run autoclave cycle
- dry, restock

After the sterilization station has been cleaned and ready for the next go-round. Prep and restock all stations followed up by the shop stations trash. During any down time, detail work around the shop is always appreciated and never goes unnoticed. But what I really like to see, is an apprentice that takes an interest in the clients design, give me an apprentice who can give a different point of view any day.

Prep work for an apprentice is how to learn the proper steps to take in order to do any procedure. It's the apprentices' job to make the work load of the artist lighter. As the apprentice, just remember;

- all the Master should have to do is sit down
- the apprentice, makes the life at the shop easier
- never touch others equipment unless otherwise instructed
- everything you've been instructed
- all required curriculum
- give it your all

As any professional, there is a certain level of personal hygiene standards. A tattoo artist has the privilege to be how they prefer to be. But even the fugliest of us all have a higher hygiene standard.

Let's start with your hands, your money makers. Keep your hands clean, clipped, and classy. By keeping your hands well groomed sets a good tone with a hardy handshake. By taking the proper care of your hands, insures the clients safety and an overall better opinion of you and your business.

The next on the checklist will be the face. Clean face, teeth, and hair, are very important for a respectable business person. If your preference is to have facial hair just keep in mind that bacteria loves hair follicles, just keep your facial hair well groomed, that goes for the hair on top of your head as well.

Third on your checklist should be work clothes. Always wear clean attire appropriate for a tattoo studio. We are subject to all types of diseases, just by following a simple rule of work clothes/dirty, and home clothes/clean. By keeping your clothes separate during wash, and other house hold items will reduce cross contamination and risk to those in your home.

The final checklist item will be scent. If you have had the pleasure of a client's B.O., then you will appreciate why our scent is a large factor on a personal level. Least of all B.O. is dried bacteria decomposing on the surface of the epidermis.

Tattoo studios must use sterilization equipment that is approved by the U.S. Food and Drug Administration. The Apprentice, Instructor, License holder and Agent must have access to the manufacturer's manual and all recommendations for operation of all units.

Each apprentice responsible for the sterilization must be able to demonstrate procedures on demand. When the authorized agent pops in to make their unscheduled inspection all employees on site must be able to demonstrate a competent application of all procedures.

After each procedure all reusable instruments must be cleaned of contaminants, blood, ink, or residue before sterilization. Sterilization packages must have approved sterilized indicator on or in each of the individual pouches.

Each package must have a date and initials of an apprentice or person sterilizing the instruments. Sterile pouches must be kept and stored in a dust-free container. The studio must keep all records of sterilization procedures for a minimum of 3 years.

The studio sterilization records should consist of:

1. date of sterilization
2. quantity and type of instruments
3. initials of individual

Each and every sterilization unit must have monthly spore test approved by a laboratory. Maintain all records of the results of spore test and keep in the studio at all times for a minimum of 3 years.

In every basic study there is an understanding of what to do, and how to do it. If all your basic knowledge in the world of tattooing is that, "the gun puts ink in the body" then I am not interested in you or your ability as a tattoo artist. If you have a humble attitude, and some desire to learn I can work with that. Like I was told I can teach skills.

Take your time in mastering each skill your Master teaches you, focus on an education and complete your goals. Set out a plan and follow that plan out and allow room for error. Not knowing it all can help, but no matter what you know, it is the credentials earned during your apprenticeship that makes it worth it.

Taking your time and mastering the skills is a great start, but not all tattoo artist careers sky-rocket to success. It's truly not how great you are as a tattoo artist, but how many times you can pick yourself up and dust yourself off and get right back in the chair for the next go round.

The life of the apprentice is not an easy life. I personally had a long and quite expensive apprenticeship. These hard times shaped my business plan, and I kept true to my goals. Taking large leaps of faith, I understood what sacrifices our family would have to take in order for our dreams to come true.

CHAPTER TWO
Tattoo Equipment

1. Parts of the tattoo machine
2. Proper set up of equipment
3. Basic needle configuration
4. Applying a proper stencil

Parts of the Tattoo Machine

Many basic components make up the mechanical, electrical magnetic systems of what is called a tattoo machine. What a complex piece of machinery and the knowledge of these systems hold many more secrets for the better of mankind, and the proper care and knowledge of the equipment will reflect in the artist work. If one part is worn out, the machine will have a hard time doing its job.

Knowledge of your machine is crucial, if you grab the wrong machine for the procedure your about to do, there is a risk of causing unnecessary damage to the epidermis, possibly causing what we call tattoo scarring, serious damage to the dermis.

When you grab a machine, make sure you know and understand your machine, if you grab a short stroke machine to do a procedure and not so sure of its purpose. You might have a difficult time getting your ink to set right in the epidermis.

What are the differences in a long stroke and a short stroke machine? What is the gap between the front spring and contact screw? A stroke is the up-down motion of the needle. An open contact is one stroke.

Knowing the right duty cycle of each of your machines is one's own preference but follow the basics of what works. As the apprentice fine tuning a machine is a hard feat to master. As lots will say "no big deal" Well until one learns the machine and how to replace all components of a handcrafted work of art, NONE SHALL PASS.

The frame is our basic starting point of a machine. The frames design is not what one should focus on when buying a machine. Rather one should know what the machine is made of, and better yet who made the machine they hold in their hand. This is what I seek out to know about the artist that thinks they know how to tattoo. Know what kind of machine you have!

Coils are a major factor in how the machine runs any inconsistency in the wire wrap or malfunction in a coil can be a time consuming process. Coils are your source of current to the electro-magnetic machine and knowing what wrap coil you have will keep you running nice and smooth for a long time.

What is a tattoo machine spring? What gage is needed? What if a machine brakes? These are all great questions to ask, and help keep the Master student relationship on course.

Parts of a machine:

Check the following components of the machine for wear and tear from use. Clean and maintain accordingly. Keeping a well-kept machine will keep you consistent.

1. Frame
2. Coils
3. Capacitor
4. Front/back springs
5. Front/back binding post
6. Contact screw
7. Armature bar
8. Clip cord
9. Foot switch
10. Power supply

Once a machine is at a duty cycle you can work with, set it and leave it.

There are a few factors that can affect the function of a tattoo machine.

1. Types of tattooing: Required speed

2. Needle configuration: Required force
3. Size of gap: Stroke length
4. Coil resistance: Affects the speed
5. Microfarad rating of capacitor: Affects the speed
6. Rubber band tension: Affects the speed
7. Weight of armature bar: control speed and force
8. Dimension of front/back springs: control speed and force
9. Angel or deflection of springs: affects force

Understanding how the machine works, and how it is put together is one of the need to knows' of tattooing. Knowing how to fine tune your machine takes experience and instruction. The only difference from a scratcher and an artist is, good work isn't cheap and cheap work isn't good.

PROPER SET UP OF EQUIPMENT

It is very important to know what you have in your hand. Make sure to handle each piece of equipment with care. One slip up can ruin a client's entire experience. Be prepared for anything and if you think you have all the bases covered, cover them again. Have back-ups and inspect all equipment before you can start a set-up.

1. Machine #1: a small liner with a stroke length of 1/16" it should run at 140Hz
2. Machine #2: a large liner with a stroke length of 3/32" it should run at 140Hz
3. Machine #3: a gray wash with a stroke length of 1/8" it should run at 135Hz
4. Machine #4: a large/color with a stroke length of 1/8" it should run at 100Hz

Start by sanitizing your area, chairs, armrest, countertop and any surface that will be utilized. Place down protective barrier on all surfaces and equipment for cross contamination precautions. If a proper set-up procedure is followed then you will cut down the chances of any spread of infection, so let's go over some basic points of the set-up.

- Glove up and sanitize the surfaces
- Glove up and set out all instruments being used during procedures
- Glove up and set up machines
- Glove up and prep the client
- Glove up and set out inks, water cups, paper towels
- Glove up and set tattoo
- Glove up after all breaks
- Glove up for aftercare
- Glove up for clean-up

Knowing the State Department of Health practices and code will not make you a better artist, but it will make sure you give a great tattoo consistently. Proper needle depth insures the life of a tattoo and a properly set tattoo will last twenty years with vibrancy.

So I go to lunch one day with my wife in Amarillo, Texas. I am looking at a young girl in line ahead of us, covered with scratchers delight from neck to toe. Most of my thoughts were about this poor young girls future, so I had to ask why she had let someone do this to her? As my wife drops an elbow down on me, she says with all the pride she could muster, "my boyfriend is a new and up-coming artist, and he does all of my work." There stood mookie, with a grin of all little beady eyed creeps. The Mook starts telling me how he was going to do very, very big things in that city. Then I found myself thinking of that poor Amarillo girl's future. The point of this story was to know what your machine does, set it up properly and find the right setting for each of your machines, your tattoo work will reflect what you know and not what you think you can do. The only one you should practice on is yourself.

BASIC NEEDLE CONFIGURATION

Tattoo needles come as a short or long taper, round liners/loose and tight, flats and magnums. The short taper needles require more force to penetrate the epidermis properly. Tattoo needles come in many various sizes and types. Let us only focus on the basic set-ups.

- For fine line work use a small configuration set-up, single to a 5trl for great fine line work
- For bold line work use a large configuration set-up, 7rl to a 14r works great bold designs
- For a great brush stroke look use a flat configuration set-up 4f to 6f works awesome grey wash
- For great color use a magnum configuration set-up 7mag t0 pack in color and perfect for blending

All needles do different tasks and learning those proper techniques for each needle configuration is how to judge the artist ability. Proper set-up and proper needle configuration is half the battle for setting a good tattoo. These are the basic tools we need to do our job, like a painter and his brush. Make sure to dispose of each needle after use, needles are single use only and belong in the sharps bio-materials container.

Basic needle configurations are as follows;

Round liners: these liners come in many sizes and range anywhere from single needle to as large and tight or loose as you dare, just don't get to nuts with it.

> Round tight; for tight groupings
> Round shader; for bolder grouping

Flats: this configuration is best used to mimic the brush stroke of a paintbrush and come in a few different sizes

> Double stack; is similar to mag's only this configuration is lined up with each other

Magnums or mag: this needle configuration is an off-set stack of needles these configurations come in many sizes. It's great to really pack in the ink.

> Curved mag; this configuration has a slight curve to it

As the apprentice you should learn and know each configuration and their primary purpose. Only after knowing what set up to use should the apprentice start making needles.

The apprentice should average twenty-five needles of two types of round configurations a day or twenty-five needles of one type of flat or mag configurations per day until this skill is mastered.

APPLYING THE STENCIL PROPERLY

As the "apprentice" I grew from many blunders, one of them was my best one yet. I had just got my chance to lay out my first stencil at the shop just a few weeks earlier, so I was still a bit excited and feeling the pressure from the big man. I had all the confidence in the world, "I got this" no worries I'm thinking. My chance for glory, I was going to shine down like the warmth of the sun. I went through my checklist twice. I was ready, nice and tacky/check.

Stencil/check
Squared/check
Ready/check
Apply/che-ch-ch-

What the . . .

I apply again just to make sure I got the stencil on and allowed enough time for the stencil to take to the skin and I pull to unveil my perfect application of a stencil, and no go, not a mark on the skin. Everyone is rolling, this has never happened to me before, and I knew the stencil was good it was all over my gloves. "What the hell?" is all I can say; with a grim disappointed expression I took a walk of shame to the back office for a new stencil, and a healthy ripping to my pride. During all the pressure I come to the reason of my calamity, as we all stood puzzled over this odd situation being reminded that "I got this" were the words I used. I had applied the stencil on backward and as my foot enters mouth, the entire shop burst out in laughter. A great chuckle and a ripping I still haven't lived down. My only advice I have is, keep an orderly routine and you will have a successful tattoo.

Let us cover some of the basic steps in applying a proper stencil

1. Wash hands and glove up
2. Clean the surface of skin
3. Shave a large area to place stencil
4. Apply tack to area
5. Square and center your stencil
6. Apply stencil and discard gloves

A stencil should set centered on the body, squared and facing forward, nicely spaced out and flows with the shape and curves of the body. Finding the setting of darkness of a stencil is the artist personal preference. As much so the stencil should be dark enough to be visible and holds to the skin. Applying a tacky film with a great stencil will give you a greater chance of a successful tattoo every time.

As a tattoo artist we have our hand in so many different fields and professions that make up our occupation, from art appreciation to medical science, from culture to history, from current affairs to foreign language. If being a "Rock Star" tattoo artist is what you truly want those I listed are just a bit of the things you must know, not including the basic requirements of the curriculum.

Understanding the mechanics of your equipment is a must, follow all manufacturers' instructions and print up log sheets the health inspector likes records of use, cleaning and test. Let's cover some basic shop equipment.

I.   Autoclave: A vessel for high pressure steam, used to sterilize instruments
II. Ultrasonic: Cleaning equipment that uses sonic pulses to clean and brake down contaminated instruments not a sterilizer of any type
III. Thermal fax: A machine used for transfer of design to stencil on carbon black copy

Each need to be cleaned regularly and deep cleaning once a month per machine. A date and sign sheet will do just fine to keep a record of what work has been done and any notes needed. Remember keep a log for; sterilizations, cleaning, and spore test. Keep your equipment in top condition and you will cut cost and produce consistent work. Everyone expects this.

Tattoo tubes, grips, and tips. There are many styles and many types. What is best? What to use? Every artist has their own style, taste and preference, the question is. How does it fit in my hand? What type of consistency do I have? Now go and find your style.

Tips are in many shapes, sizes and styles. Grips are great today many styles, colors and designs that puts just enough character into who you are as an artist. Tips are getting better and better, I personally like small rounds, large diamonds and open face mag. As for my grip I prefer a 1" grip. The weight of my grips and the balance of my machine play a role when choosing proper equipment.

Staying consistent is the key and practice the techniques necessary to skillfully apply a tattoo, focus on being the best at what you do. Practice on paper, canvas, fruit, fake skin before you ever tap on live skin.

The source of your machines power comes from the power supply. Not all power supplies are the same but they all do the main function and that is to run a machine. The power supply and connections is the preference of the artist. As long as you have a solid connection you will have a greater chance at performing and applying a tattoo.

If you have to trouble-shoot any machine problems, start with your connections. Contact points get a carbon build up, just keep clean and your machine will run smooth. Then work the machine down the line, springs, coils and capacitor.

If all is good, work your clip cord down to the power supply, if necessary switch out foot switch, clip cord, or power supply, until you get a chance to diagnose your problem, if you are capable of repairing properly then fix and move on, if not order new equipment.

It's a great idea to have a few back-ups ready to go, what can go wrong, will go wrong.

Choose your power supply wisely or make costly mistakes later. Update your equipment every 4-8 years or as needed. Stay on top of your game, keep it clean. Never sacrifice price over quality, and protect your investments.

CHAPTER THREE
Medical Procedures

1. Basic review of terminology
2. Proper health code procedures
3. Braking down and sterilization
4. Station set up and tattoo prep

Every tattoo studio, shop, gallery, etc. has certain medical procedures they perform. It is the most important part of being a tattoo artist, not only keeping the health and safety of your clients from bacteria or viruses, but also how to know what to look for, to understand the types of skin conditions and when to tattoo and when not to.

- What type of skin condition are you working with
- How is the blood flow
- Where are moles or other blemishes
- How much pressure to apply
- How far to stretch the skin
- How deep does the needle travel
- How fast does a needle travel

These are questions you will be faced with and be expected to know, if you have no clue or care to understand then you are not ready to be the tattoo artist. See to me there is more to tattooing than drawing on someone's body, it is not just the art form but more toward health science and that's the field you have chosen, Blood, Gore, Pain, "it kicks ass".

Every state varies in health code procedures but universal precautions stand strong in a great tattoo studio, and they should all have a great standing with the health department and health inspector. A quality studio focuses on their health practice as well as the quality of work that comes from that studio.

Now from shop to shop you will find all ways to get the same end result. Not all studios do the same procedures but by all standards we all practice the basic precautions to apply or administer any, body modification.

Required documents, licensing and certificates are needed to lawfully and legally perform a tattoo. The knowledge needed should be taught to you or you might have to do a bit of leg work of your own to find out this information.

Basic steps to follow; Glove up

Never forget a pair of gloves. Universal precautions basically instruct how to protect, wrap, cover and clean. If you follow your basic steps to stay safe, stay clean, you will stay in business.

Keep single use instruments to their one basic function and discard properly in a medical waste, or bio-material, or sharps containers, these containers are on a pick-up and delivery service for a fee. Any and all bio-waste materials are labeled and properly for disposal. Be a professional and take responsibility with bio-waste and all sharps' material.

As a tattoo artist it will be your final decision whether or not to perform a tattoo. Either understand, what you're what you are tattooing, or take the risk of not knowing what you are looking at. If you're not sure and you haven't found enough efficient documentation and you still question, stay safe, stay clear. By asking to set an appointment or ask to see how well a blemish clears-up in a few days. Try to be polite. Even suggest another placement.

Take an interest in what you do by knowing how it's done. Watch your Master for hours of tattoos observe how they work the tattoo. See where their hands are placed and find out why. If you find your instructor gabbing with their client more than usual, rather than advancing your apprenticeship, it is time to find more constructive things to do than standing in the light. Got time to lean, got time to clean.

Time to get your study on . . .

Out of all the states I've studied, the more strict states were Virginia, and Florida. I like Virginia's State code on tattooing best. I suggest to be apprenticed under these state guidelines of apprentice curriculum. This credited apprenticeship criteria is a professional standard of this industry. This is an excellent standard to base all apprenticeship guidelines. If you do well enough, one day you might get the chance to run or even own an ink slinging shop of your own one day.

Each state has different health code procedures that include client qualifications, disclosures, and all record keeping. Properly file all invoices according to that state. Follow all instruction according to the shop you work for, gain exposure as an apprentice and be professional. You will make a great tattoo artist.

BASIC REVIEW OF TERMINOLOGY

Some basic terminology the apprentice uses in the course of ones' day:

- Germicidal soap
- Types of bacteria
- Types of virus
- Layers of skin
- Universal precautions
- Types of machines

When the apprentice can answer any question thrown their way, they just might be ready to start a tattoo career. Cover all standards of all procedures before you can proclaim yourself a tattoo artist. There is something to a starving artist don't take your struggle or success lightly. Be proud but be humble this is the nature of the tattoo gods.

How well can the apprentice cover the parts of the machine?

- What is the capacitor
- Name the machines parts
- Name needle configurations
- Name the ink being used
- Walk through a complete set-up

Most individuals out there in the tattoo world looking or just starting out, has little to no knowledge of any equipment they use, or has hardly any knowledge of medical procedures necessary to perform these procedures.

If you don't know what it is in your hand or anything about the machine you're holding, if you have no clue of medical practice, how the hell do you know how to use it? This is a geek off the street, and that apprenticeship is a whole different school of hard knocks all together. It is not about how you got started tattooing, it's all about perfecting the skill and technical abilities along with a level of professionalism one gains from a respectable career.

The Master needs to know if anything fails. From point of trouble shooting to repair time should take no longer than 30 minutes, any longer than that and be prepared for more than just a loss of wages. Word of mouth is a burning fire. Know how to control the fire or, the flames will swallow up everyone around you.

Apprenticeship program: an approved tattoo training program

Apprentice sponsor: an individual approved to conduct tattooing apprenticeship training program

Aseptic technique: a hygienic practice that prevents the direct transfer of microorganisms

Direct supervision: licensee shall be present in the shop at all times when services are being performed by an apprentice

Endorsement: a method of obtaining a license by a person who is currently licensed in another state

Licensee: person, partnership, etc. holding a license issued by a state

Reinstatement: having a license restored to effectiveness after the expiration date has passed

Renewal: continuing the effectiveness of license for another time period

Sterilization area: a separate room or area separate from workstations with restricted client access in which instruments are cleaned

Tattoo Instructor: a person who has been certified, who meets competency standards as an instructor

These terms already should be a part of the apprentice vocabulary. Listed below are terms to become familiar with, and understand any and all terms required of you.

Apprentice curriculum required terms

Microbiology: microscopic organisms

Immunization: protection against disease

Disinfect: to cleanse

Safety: not causing injury

Tattoo: practice of marking the skin by inserting pigments

Tattoo laws and regulations: standards of practice for tattoo artist

Blood: consisting of plasma in witch red and white blood cells are suspended

Contaminate: to make impure by contact

Apprentice curriculum required terms

These are types of microorganisms, viruses, bacteria and fungi. Knowledge of these terms, are mandatory, understanding how to visually assess a client because most will not disclose their medical history to you.

Organism	Responsible for
Hepatitis B, C	Hepatitis
H.I.V.	AIDS
Herpes simplex	Cold sores
Herpes B	Encephalomyelitis
Influenza	flu
Pneumococci pneumonia	Mycoplasma Pneumonia
Escherichia Coli	Wound infection, wound care
Klebsiella pneumonia	Secondary invader
Proteus Mirabilis	Acne, suppurating wounds
Mycobacterium tuberculosis	Turberculosis
Staphlococcus pyrogenes	Boils, abcesses
Staphlococcus aureus	Boils, carbuncies, furundes
Streptococcus vividans	Normal flora of mouth but causes subacute endocarditis

Some medical conditions are really hard to detect, others are virtually impossible. Now don't expect everyone to tell you what is medically wrong with them for some, you might be there awhile. Try to get the clients information on your disclosure/waiver forms. No one needs to know the true nature of ones' health except the artist and the client.

Giving your clients a safe environment to relax in while getting their body work finished, will grow great confidence in your studio and build an awesome reputation.

PROPER HEALTH CODE PROCEDURES

For the apprentice this is simple cover, wrap, protect. Nothing gets used during a procedure without the proper protection. Most of all remember to wash your hands before starting and after stopping. Knowing proper hand washing technique will come as second nature, if not you might struggle. Not a thing gets used from my station without surface to surface contact barriers that protects from cross contamination. Learn and practice these proper procedures set by O.S.H.A. during your apprenticeship, bad habits are hard to brake.

Now after the all procedures are finished and it's time to clean the area, bandage it properly, explain the proper after care of the new tattoo. Try to draw back on your own experience, in similar locations and don't ask them how bad it hurt, if you want to know, get one in that location and find out first hand.

It has been said pain is an illusion, or pain is in the mind. Now don't go preaching this either, you will just be made to look like a fool. No matter what you've heard or what people say about tattoos going numb, haven't committed themselves fully to a large piece, and argue all you like; TATTOOS-HURT. It hurts just enough, this is what makes them so enjoyable.

Treat all body fluids from every person as potentially infectious. Follow the recommendations of a blood borne pathogens exposure control plan. A blood borne pathogens exposure control plan should include:

- Various levels of risk of employees that may have occupational exposure
- Training requirements
- Work practice controls

- Engineering controls
- Procedures for an exposure incident

Tattoo artist are subjected to all types of bacteria and viruses, it is important to have a high standard of hygiene just to protect your home life. Wash and properly discard all soiled work clothes of the day separately from all other house hold clothing.

Make sure to shower before any interaction with family members. Try to keep hand contact to a minimum, we live in a hand shake society but as a tattoo artist a forearm bump is good enough. Be aware of what you touch and mindful of where you place your hands, keep yourself safe and you'll find no problem providing a safe environment for your clients.

Most standards of shops health procedures fall solely on the instruction of the Master. If this portion of your education is lacking or falls short of the curriculum, seek out the knowledge you need there is no excuse for the lack of education.

To build an understanding of this trade, you must be responsible for yourself and test your abilities. Go just a bit further, pushing past perception and be better than the one you call Master. Gained and shared knowledge makes one great.

Brake Down and Sterilization

Start every brake down the same way every time to get a consistent routine. Glove up and follow a routine you are comfortable with, as long as that it gets the job done. Now a brake-down can be or get very messy and not everyone has the best sense of containment needed to be considered clean. Not all shops are spotless but the point is to do more: more for me and my future, more than the minimum.

Cleanup procedures

- Mix all cleaning solutions properly and according to manufacturers' directions
- Use personal protective equipment
- Use manufacturer directions from a body fluid spill kit
- Remove visible materials with absorbent towel
- Spray disinfectant on contaminated area and let stand for several minutes
- Once the area has been disinfected, dry area with absorbent towel and discard properly
- Discard all sharp materials in the appropriate manner

Glove removal

- Grip one glove near the cuff and peel it down until it comes off inside out. Cup glove in the palm of your gloved hand
- Place two fingers of your bare hand inside the cuff of the remaining glove
- Peel that glove down so that it too comes off inside out and over the first glove
- Properly dispose of the gloves

Wash your hands

- Wet your hands and apply liquid, bar, or powder soap
- Rub hands together vigorously to make a lather and scrub all surfaces
- Continuing for 30-45 seconds!
- Rinse hands well under water
- Dry your hands using a paper towel or air dryer
- If possible, use the towel to turn off the faucet

This is for anyone who needs the reminder. Keep your booth clean daily. Nobody wants to sit in a dirty chair or see the dirty sink. If your trash is full, take it out. No one wants to look at bio-waste, especially if it is not their waste. When the booths, gallery, front desk, and restrooms have a clean appeal to them; clients feel safe, and believe it or not this is great advertisement.

Try not to make more of a mess as you clean. Keep your cross contamination and handling of any utensils used during a procedure in one general location. Try to keep from spilling for any unnecessary sanitation duties. Work on a single task at a time and know how to prioritize any hazardous conditions.

If all goes well during brake down and transfer of all used utensils are properly transported to the sterilization station. Every instrument and utensils have to be scrubbed, cleaned, washed, packaged, sterilized and logged.

Follow your own routine that gets the job done just keep in mind the apprentice is there to make the job of the Master easier. It is the apprentice who should stay on top of all sanitation duties. Now go clean the restroom.

How to reduce your risk

- Do not eat, drink, smoke, apply cosmetics or handle contact lenses in areas where there is a possibility of exposure to blood borne pathogens
- When emptying trash containers, do not use your hands to compress the trash in the bag
- Lift and carry trash away from body
- Follow procedures for handling laundry
- Keep contaminated laundry separate from other laundry
- Needles and other sharps must be discarded in bio-containers

Bodily fluids, especially those visibly contaminated with blood, have the potential to transmit disease. Casual contact like a handshake, hugging, sharing food, doorknobs, etc. is prime breading grounds for infection. If you think you've been exposed, document, and report. Seek medical attention and evaluation. Then follow up as needed.

By understanding what to look for and how to spot potential dangers, you will reduce your risk of exposure to communicable diseases. Potential terminal diseases are the daily risks of a tattoo artist. Stay alert, Stay safe, Stay alive.

Aftercare of a new tattoo

The client's aftercare is a procedure that requires verbal and written instructions. As an apprentice you must be able to verbally instruct the client in the proper care, cleaning, of all aspects of precautions of care for a new tattoo.

The written instructions of after care of a new tattoo should consist of when to consult with a health care practitioner, all phone numbers of importance, name of all involved. Follow the list of basic instruction for at least two weeks.

1. Minimize sun exposure
2. No soaking in tub or swimming of any kind
3. How to properly clean a new tattoo

Make sure to take the proper precautions when instructing the client, provide them with all the necessary information about the aftercare of the tattoo, the names and phone numbers of the studio and artist performing the procedure. If the apprentice can provide a reassuring hand to the client with a departure package of after care and contact advertisement, the client will be more perceptive to the apprentice in the future.

Station Set-Up and Tattoo Prep.

Sacred ground a tattoo booth can be. Balanced by Feng shui or taboo swag, whatever your custom may be. Pay respect to the tattoo gods however that may be. Some booths have a mythical prospective and this is what gives the shop its character. Remember only 1/3 of your public will agree with your taste. Finding a natural décor will give you a better feel of what the public wants.

The station must have non-porous surfaces, countertops with sink, shelves, trash, sharps container, glove rack, equipment shelves, chairs and lights. Knowing what a booth requires for all proper procedures will give a great impression to any patron that is paying for their service, and build confidence in the shop.

Understanding how to set-up is one of the last steps before you get to tattoo. The apprentice must completely put a machine together. The apprentice must successfully place a stencil. The apprentice must complete a successful set-up and brake-down procedure. The apprentice must have a practical use of knowledge in all required curriculum.

Only after a skills checklist has been completed, will an apprentice follow under the watchful eye of the Master, they might get the opportunity to set some ink on a willing test subject.

Let us see what you have learned by watching your Master. Set-up the tattoo booth properly and after you have explained the procedures to the client, this helps them understand our process and reassures our competency of our job and sets the client at ease. Make sure to completely follow the steps properly for a successful set-up.

Set the station up best to fit you and your work environment. I prefer to work left to right/clean to dirty. I don't expect you to understand my set-up. I do expect you to find a set-up that is right for you.

What is tattoo prep? And why are you to prep for a tattoo? If the apprentice can give a competent answer, maybe it's time to throw a dog a bone. After the tattoo station set-up is ready all the equipment had been covered, protected, wrapped and the client has been prepped and shaved. The apprentice has set a proper stencil. Check and double check your list. All that should remain is for the artist to sit in the chair. Now would be a good time to ask the Master for approval to perform the procedure.

CHAPTER FOUR
Basic Skills Checklist

1. Procedures
2. Sanitation Station
3. Health procedures and terminology
4. Maintenance
5. Personal Hygiene

The Basic skills of the apprentice, is the knowledge of what to do, when to do it and why it needs to be done. By asking the five W's, why, who, what, when, where. You can answer most questions thrown your way.

Follow all standards that are required by your location. All the necessary information will come into your hands; it is what you do with this knowledge, which determines how successful you will be.

Knowing how to cover the basic information and keeping the basic outline of apprenticeships true to the nature of Master and Student. Providing, a professional standard, a consistent curriculum for your apprentice full potential.

Hand washing procedures for tattooing

1. Wet hands and wrist with warm running water
2. Apply a sufficient amount of soap to open palms
3. Move hands away from running water, lather and scrub well
4. Wash hands well for about 45 seconds
5. Scrub between fingers, back of each hand and palm to palm
6. Scrub fingertips
7. Scrub wrist
8. Rinse thoroughly under warm water
9. Dry hands well, do not shake
10. Turn off faucet with paper towel

Clients Records

All client records must be filed and saved at the tattoo studio for a minimum of 3 years. These records are to be accessible for review by any agent or lead artist. Disclosure of clients medical conditions, are to ensure the healing process of an invasive procedure.

The following client information must be documented.

1. Allergies or reaction to latex, pigments, dyes, disinfectants, soaps or metals
2. Anticoagulants
3. Diabetes
4. Hemophilia
5. Skin diseases or lesions or any type of skin damage

The following client consent form must include

1. Name of the client
2. Address and current phone #
3. Date of procedure
4. Design
5. Placement of procedure
6. Artist performing procedure
7. Cost of procedure
8. Waiver of right to seek any damages, relieve all involved of any responsibility

These are the most important parts of the clients consent forms, follow a good structure and make sure all involved are pleased with any product that walks out of your studio and you will never find yourself in drama.

PROCEDURES

Shop:

Daily: Weekly: Monthly:

Every shop has daily duties knowing what they are and when to perform them is essential. By keeping a standard log sheet, will keep the maintenance cost down, and the more detailed a shop is the larger the client flow. Weekly duties are for keeping up on inventory and light clean sweep of the shop.

Monthly procedures will cover most deep cleaning of the shops equipment, stations, and proper arrangement of the shops décor. File all client documents and any records or logs that might be required. The monthly art work produced must be filed properly. Any inventory orders, receipts, and any nature of such, must be properly documented for future use. Keeping the shop stocked and clean sets the standard for the next apprentice.

If the apprentice has no format this would be the perfect chance to push incentive. Show that you have interest in being there and you're not just a floater. The apprentice is expected to take responsibility for the care of the shop by creating log forms for all stations and checklist for shop duties. This will give the apprentice a better understanding of the routine of a shop. This is a great way to build the confidence of the apprentice.

Tattoo booth:

Daily: Weekly: Monthly:

Every artist likes their booth just the way they are, so never mess with the booth décor or equipment unless told otherwise. Even though the booth must be cleaned daily, every day, every tattoo, every free time there are things to be done in a booth. Make sure you leave the booth as it is, no one should even know you were there. What you do with your booth will determine whom the cliental will be and how you want them to view you. This is your only chance to give a visual representation of who you are.

By following a checklist you have created the format and any log sheet that provides detailed documentation for inspection. Making inspection so much simpler for all involved can get you right back to work.

Once a week, is the perfect time for an inventory check, or maintenance of equipment and a detailed cleaning of the booth. Staying on top of your equipment and inventory keeps you ready for the next day, month and for many years to come.

Find time monthly for all detailed cleaning. Keep a booth dust free, stocked with all utensils. Check the bio-containers. Never get to sloppy and try to keep a safe environment.

SANITATION STATION

Daily: _____ Weekly: _____ Monthly: _____

Every section of a tattoo studio must be properly sanitized that goes with the sterilization station. Most medical equipment comes with directions on how to clean follow all the instructions of the manufacturer during any maintenance of the equipment.

Daily record keeping of all use of equipment, the daily cleaning of the counter top surface, sink and the proper cleaning of this area must have some type of daily log.

Weekly sterilization of the medical equipment and documents of the proper paper work for the health inspectors must be filed.

All monthly test records must be filed. Any station inventory and supply checklist must be filled out and ready for the Master.

State Health Department requires a strict log book and documentation of clients. Keeping on top of all forms and proper filing is perfect for the apprentice. All the license holder and inspector will have to do is check the log books.

HEALTH PROCEDURES AND TERMINOLOGY

All an apprentice needs to have is the basic instruction and knowledge of basic health procedures and the terminology. It is not enough to know how to tattoo only. It is very important that the tattoo artist knows exactly what they doing.

Now as you can tell this is not a how to tattoo guide. But the structure of this guide can make a shop run more efficient and stronger. It can make a good apprentice, a great apprentice. It can provide a sound shop structure for your apprentice curriculum.

The best part of this guide is that it can be customized to perfectly design your own structure, to meet each shops demand and a consistent curriculum platform.

Follow the terms and definitions as a starting point after that work on anatomy and health science.

Cover the microorganism transmission cycle. The apprentice must have a clear understanding of all blood borne pathogens and an understanding of the parts and functions of the layers of skin. The apprentice should have a minimum of 350 hours of instruction on this curriculum alone.

The second the apprentice is familiar with this basic knowledge, start the apprentice on sanitation and disinfectant, as well as the safety of the shop standards, followed up with professional standards.

Cover definitions of terms with a competent review and proper procedure demonstration. Make sure the apprentice can cover the proper needle care and safety practices. Make sure the apprentice provides a first-aid and CPR certificate, and any other requirements one must have to be a tattoo artist.

Finally spend a minimum of 1000 hours of instruction on the proper techniques, handling, machine construction, client forms and art portfolio. After all basics are fully covered, then the apprentice must perform a minimum of 100 tattoos at the standards of the Master and the studio. There is much more to tattooing than just putting ink in the skin.

The knowledge of what to recognize and what to expect, while assessing a potential client, will give the tattoo artist a lower risk of infection. This is how to properly and professionally apply the tattoo, and when to properly and professionally turn your clients away.

You will need an education on the physical human anatomy and how altering the body will have a long lasting effect on that individual. It is about the true mental state of your client, and why the client is having a procedure done. This will help you understand what you do and why tattoo artist do this job. Try knowing what to look for when weeding out potential risks.

Now being a tattoo artist isn't all fame and glory, but knowledge is power and the more you implement into a structure the more successful ones career will be.

Tattoo studios are under health department regulations and to fall short of the proper education or experience will hinder any apprentice from becoming a Journeyman tattoo artist.

How to understand what is a potential risk.

HIV and AIDS

HIV attacks your body's ability to fight against disease and causes AIDS. Symptoms may or may not be apparent. Someone can be infected for years and never know. Only a blood test can confirm the infection.

Common symptoms are:

- Fever
- Fatigue
- Weight Loss
- Rash

HIV is a fragile virus that dies within seconds outside of the body. Depending on the amount of HIV present in the body fluid and conditions will determine how long the virus will live. HIV is prominently spread through sexual contact or by sharing needles/syringes with an infected person. HIV is not spread by casual contact.

Hepatitis B

Hepatitis B virus also known as HBV—reproduces in the liver which causes inflammation and possibly cirrhosis or liver cancer. Symptoms may or may not be apparent. Only a blood test can confirm the infection.

Common Symptoms are:

- Jaundice
- Fatigue
- Nausea, loss of appetite
- Dark urine
- Joint pain
- Clay colored bowels
- Abdominal discomfort

HBV can live outside of the body for up to 7 days or longer. HBV is primarily spread by sexual contact, sharing needles/syringes and sharps exposures on the job. HBV is not spread by casual contact. There is a vaccine available given in 3 doses over a period of 6 months.

Hepatitis C

Hepatitis C also known as HCV reproduces in the liver which causes inflammation and possibly cirrhosis or liver cancer. Symptoms may or may not be apparent. Only a blood test can confirm the infection.

HCV is primarily spread by sharing needles/syringes, transfusion or transplant of an infected donor and by tattoos. There is no cure or vaccination.

Maintenance

The ability to maintain all shop equipment is the secrets we share with very few. When I got started I was told one thing by so many different tattoo artists. The knowledge that has to be taught is not free. I hope I stayed true to our profession.

The studio must keep the records of all maintenance, sterilization, tattoos, cleaning duties, and filed properly. Not only do you have to be aware of health and safety procedures, a routine building check is good to keep your building up to code. The structure of the building is the everyday checklist, besides the obvious, the electrical, the plumbing and all interior and exterior lights and signs.

Keep in mind cheap isn't best and best isn't cheap, but find a great compromise buying the best doesn't mean paying the most.

Log sheets for daily, weekly, monthly, and annual formats will drive cost down and maximize profit potential.

Break down the stations of the shop and follow the routine you're comfortable with. Design a simple format of checklist and log sheets with a description, signature and date. For the best lay-out use e-forms, make the studio as paperless as possible or print and store caveman style, "mmm me need toner".

It is time to test the apprentice. Take a few standard questions, and have them show practical use.

Does the apprentice know how to completely reassemble a tattoo machine and name the parts of a tattoo machine?

Can the apprentice complete shop routines, daily, weekly, or monthly task on demand or when needed?

Can the apprentice trouble shoot the equipment or fix any shop malfunctions?

How well can the apprentice explain after care of the tattoo?

What spot does the apprentice fill?

A struggling artist will struggle but a tattoo artist will complete any shop needs, cover every section and completes a consistent routine, every time. This is what I call a professional standard.

PERSONAL HYGIENE

Grooming Techniques are a personal standard as a professional, being groomed accordingly is not a necessity but it is a respectful practice.

Start with hands the head and finally clothing and appearance. Just stay clean and fresh and you'll get a better response.

If the artist is dirty the client feels dirty. If the client is dirty this will make the shop dirty. If the shop looks dirty clients think the artist is dirty. The shop will not do well if the shop has the reputation as a "pig pen".

This goes for your clients as well. Do what you will but I prefer a clean canvas to work with. I have no problem rejecting a client for their personal hygiene issues.

If the tattoo is that important, then demand some level of respect and personal hygiene from your clients, they demand the best from you and your work.

Basic common sense is the best practice when it comes to personal hygiene. The culture of the shop will vary. Perhaps the nature of the shop may be a relaxed dress code, and other shops might have a strict dress code. Whatever is required of the apprentice apparel, the most important thing to know is how to adapt to your environment or predict the taste or style of the clients. This will sky rocket the apprentices' status in a shop.

Like my baseball coach told us right before handing out jerseys, "If you look good, you will play well." I firmly believe in choosing the proper apparel that projects confidence and appears professional. Be yourself but have some class. Your appearance is a huge impression for a potential client. Stay Clean, stay healthy and stay working.

CHAPTER FIVE
Apprentice Structure

1. Daily shop duties
2. Weekly duties of the apprentice
3. Apprentice monthly responsibilities
4. Common apprenticeships

Most shops have a tight ship when it comes to how to train the apprentice, keeping a consistent format is the key to a successful apprenticeship. Not all shops have a standard structured curriculum to complete an apprenticeship following a simple structure and format your personal standards will give the apprentice what they are paying for, a Professional Education.

If being an apprentice is all you want in life, then be sure that those that share your life are on board. This just might not be everything is seems to be and in a heartbeat it can be taken away.

Be professional, be true to yourself, be ready for the worst and be strong.

Daily Shop Duties

The shop daily duties should be second nature by the apprentice before they are accepted as an apprentice. All basics of cleaning are common knowledge and do not need much training or explanation of how to do.

One of the most important parts of the apprenticeship is proper documentation and proper filing of all forms by keeping a daily review of all shop duties at the least. The most efficient shops have daily log sheets that document the what, who, and when of all the daily duties.

The better the shop stays on track with daily routines and completes a standard checklist for all stations, will help keep the shop clean, safe, and full of clients. The more detailed the checklist the less to worry about.

Most tattoo shops have these daily duties always move the furniture and clean behind the décor.

Start with the common area the gallery or wherever it is where patrons gather. Create a checklist, skills sheet, or a log book to cover all daily routines, and make sure to cover 3 Xs over throughout the course of the day. Keep a good stock ready for a smooth transition nothing is worse than looking like a dud if the equipment, supply, or utensils run out, and now no one can produce. That means what wise guy? That means I am not happy. If you cost the shop money you might be expected to find a way to cover the cost.

Now most shops start with the floors and this should be the last item on your list. All dust particles fall and settle on the floor, dust is made up of dead skin cells mostly. So do the floors last and allow the floors to dry properly. Try not to let traffic on the wet floor.

If floors are last and dust particles fall and settle what do you think suits your shop best by starting first.

Daily duties

First assess the shop from top to bottom. If a shop will take the twenty minutes it needs to create a short list of duties. That shop will stay in tip top shape.

The list should be from celling to floor, daily through weekly duties. Make sure your list has a place for name, date, and a spot to keep detailed notes.

The celling is the most neglected zone in a tattoo studio, you know we are always looking down at our work so much, and this can disappoint some clients. It takes very little time to do if maintained.

Large glass windows, shelves, any large standing items need to be moved and cleaned under and behind, all countertops, flash racks, art books, table tops and under all furniture in the shop.

If you have time to tattoo take time to keep your shop clean, if you can't handle the responsibility hire a cleaning crew to keep your shop in a professional standard working order.

As you sweep keep all dust piles in workable sections. Mop in overlapping sweeps from right to left and from front to back of shop. Never use mop water from station to station that is cross contamination. The general area should be mopped as needed but at least once a week. The following is a basic outline of duties and logs that should be performed but are not limited to what is listed below.

Temple Garden Tattoo

Daily/Weekly Checklist	Log Sheets	Clean/Restock/Order Forms
Spot clean ceiling	Tattoo Booths	Tattoo equipment
Shelves	Sterilization	Office supply
Counters/Sinks	Restroom	Sanitation
Tables/Chairs	Front Desk	Sterilization
Flash racks/Books	Back office	Front desk
Windows/Glass	Sanitation	Art supply
Mirrors		
Sweep		
Mop		
Trash		

WEEKLY DUTIES OF THE APPRENTICE

If this wasn't enough work for one person expect more. The weekly work order will eventually determine your pay salary or commission. So keep in mind what you absorb and what you discard might keep you from the success you might have thought you were going to have.

As an apprentice, you might find yourself at the mercy of the instructor. Never the less, not all apprenticeships are walks in the park. So know what you are getting into before you agree to just anything.

Temple garden Tattoo
weekly duties

Art: Curriculum: Shop:

- Advertisement: When you put it out there you are taking on assignments. Do not sit in the shop corner and expect clients to come to you.
- Art work: As the apprentice a strong art portfolio can give you a little credibility and it is a great start.
- Taking on the clients: Let the client know who you are, what you can do, and be reassuring that it is only the art work you are looking to design for your portfolio, and the tattoo artist will do the tattoo. This can be an apprentice way to make a bit of cash, and get your name started. Keep all art work for your portfolio, and watch your ability grow.
- Weekly curriculum: Make sure to cover the basics throughout the course of one's week.
- Making needles configurations: We've come a long ways from single use needles to cross contamination procedures.

- Shop equipment: The practical use of all equipment
- Shops daily duties: This job is endless.
- Log, document, file all required forms
- Test, file and document all medical equipment
- Routine inventory checklist

These are just the basics; an instructor will determine how in depth the apprenticeship will be. Not all instructors are the same some will focus on the art, others will focus on the mechanics of the machine, whatever the general curriculum of the apprenticeship the structure is basically the same.

Provide homework for the apprentice set deadlines for completion. All apprentice, must prove some degree of passion for doing the job that the apprentice has to do before the instructor will ever give the apprentice the opportunity to tattoo.

Apprentice Monthly Duties

If all skilled checklists have been followed and completed then the monthly duties are as simple as restocking and prep work and easy detail cleaning. If all goes well for you, the shops maintenance routine will ensure a clean and safe environment to tattoo in at all times.

Monthly log records, waivers and any document of any type must be filed properly and stored accordingly.

All custom art work must be separated into categories and by artist. All art must be filed or scanned for future reference.

The apprentice will be expected to do whatever they are instructed. If the apprentice shop assignment is advertisement and the apprentice must pass out fliers in a 75 mile radius then the apprentice will be expected to do so. Strict demands and out of your element assignments is what the apprentice is expected to cope with.

The monthly routine is a great time to check inventory and restock on any low items for the shops daily routines.

As the apprentice is learning how the shop functions on a daily schedule this will give the Master an idea of how much time the apprentice will have to complete all task. Once an apprentice finds their flow, routine, groove what have you, as long as the work gets finished the shop will stay on track.

In keeping the tradition of Master and Student as a sacred tradition, not all apprenticeships are equal and understanding the basic knowledge of being a tattoo artist should be left up to the instructor.

Take the time to refresh your own skills while creating your apprentice monthly test/worksheets, if you are going to be a Master then set the best example and the highest standards. Make sure the knowledge you have is properly instructed, so the history of the tattoo Masters legacy is pure to the nature of each generation of tattoo artist.

Being consistent and the having a level of professional standards is how you as a tattoo artist will be judged.

COMMON APPRENTICESHIPS

As an apprentice you should be building up a portfolio to show your growth in your abilities as an artist. The apprentice must work on a variety of styles and mediums, and focus on finely executed line work.

An apprentice should become familiar with past and current tattoo artist of the tattoo world. Finding similar styles and learning techniques is a great way to further your cause and show that you are more than a common tattoo artist wannabe.

If you are not nurturing a money tree then I suggest saving a nice nest egg because working a full-time job on top of an apprenticeship is pushing it a bit hard. It is best to start saving in advance of becoming an apprentice. It will most likely be a long unpaid sacrifice for quite a while.

The apprentice must shadow their instructor for a few months to get the feel of how to properly set-up the equipment for the artist to tattoo the client.

Next start cleaning the instruments of the instructor this will give the apprentice a feel for how the machine feels in the hand. Make sure all proper procedures are covered thoroughly.

Even if the apprentice has performed tattoos or has tattooed a few times, the Master or instructor will decide when the apprentice is ready for the "show", until then keep a humble attitude and be grateful for the opportunity.

The apprentice must have a solid understanding of the basic curriculum requirements of tattooing. Give every apprentice the best education by providing a consistent curriculum and a professional standard, you as a Master, demands of your apprentice.

After the completion of apprenticeship guidelines and structure of the apprenticeships curriculum, the apprentice may graduate to the next level. Now starts a new journey, good luck and try to keep our trade true to the nature of the traditional standards passed down through generations.

Every tattoo artist must provide the owner/license holder with the following.

1. Completion of Hep. B vaccine
2. First-aid certificate
3. C.P.R. certified
4. OSHA Blood borne pathogens standards
5. State required identification
6. Home phone
7. Home address
8. Full legal name
9. Social security number

A TWO YEAR APPRENTICESHIP REQUIRED CURRICULUM

Hours of instruction of curriculum and performances

- A minimum of 1500 hours of curriculum, and 100 successful tattoo performances

  350 hours devoted to the theory and curriculum in the following sections:

Microbiology:

1. Microorganisms: Viruses, Bacteria, fungi
2. Transmission cycle of infectious diseases
3. Characteristics of antimicrobial agents

Immunization:

1. Types of immunizations
2. Hepatitis A-G transmission and immunization
3. H.I.V. and Aids
4. Tetanus, streptococcal, zoonotic, tuberculosis, pneumococcal, and influenza
5. Measles, mumps and rubella
6. Vaccines and immunizations
7. General preventative measures to be taken to protect tattooist and client

Safety:

1. Proper needle handling and disposal
2. Avoid over exposer to chemicals
3. How to use the M.D.A. (material, safety, data)
4. Bio and blood spill procedures

5. Equipment and instrument storage
6. First aide and C.P.R

Blood borne pathogens standards:

1. O.S.H.A. and C.D.C. standards
2. Control plan for plan for tattooist
3. Exposure control plan for tattooist
4. Overview of compliance requirements
5. Disorders and when not to service a client

Professional standards:

1. History of tattooing
2. Business ethics
3. Record keeping: Client consent form, client health history, H.I.P.P.A.A. standards
4. Preparing a station, making appointments, parlor ethics
5. Parlor management: Licensing requirements, Taxes
6. Supplies: Usages, storage, ordering

A TWO YEAR APPRENTICESHIP
REQUIRED CURRICULUM

Hours of instruction of curriculum and performances

- A minimum of 1500 hours of curriculum, and 100 successful tattoo performances

  350 hours devoted to the theory and curriculum in the following sections:

Anatomy:

1. Understanding the skin
2. Parts of and the function of the skin

   Tattooing laws and regulations:

   150 hours devoted to the curriculum in the following section:

Sanitation and disinfection:

1. Definition of terms: sterilization; disinfection and disinfectant; sterilizer; antiseptic; germicide; decontamination; sanitation
2. Steam sterilization equipment and techniques
3. Chemical agents: antiseptic and disinfection
4. Sanitation equipment and procedures
5. Post service sanitation procedures

   1000 hours devoted to the practical training in section:

Tattooing:

1. Client consultation

2. Client heath form
3. Client disclosure
4. Client preparation
5. Sanitation and safety precautions
6. Implement of section and use
7. Proper use of and handling of equipment
8. Material selection and use
9. Ink
10. Machine: Construction; Adjustment; Power supply
11. Needles: Configuration, and making of needles
12. Art
13. Portfolio

100 successful tattoo performances:

A FOUR YEAR APPRENTICESHIP REQUIRED CURRICULUM

Hours of instruction of curriculum and performance

- A minimum of an additional 750 hours of curriculum, and 100 successful tattoo performances

  350 hours devoted to the theory and curriculum in the following sections:

Microbiology:

1. Microorganisms: Viruses, Bacteria, fungi
2. Transmission cycle of infectious diseases
3. Characteristics of antimicrobial agents

Immunization:

1. Types of immunizations
2. Hepatitis A-G transmission and immunization
3. H.I.V. and Aids
4. Tetanus, streptococcal, zoonotic, tuberculosis, pneumococcal, and influenza
5. Measles, mumps and rubella
6. Vaccines and immunizations
7. General preventative measures to be taken to protect tattooist and client

Safety:

1. Proper needle handling and disposal
2. Avoid over exposer to chemicals
3. How to use the M.D.A. (material, safety, data)
4. Bio and blood spill procedures

5. Equipment and instrument storage
6. First-aid and C.P.R

Blood borne pathogens standards:

1. O.S.H.A. and C.D.C. standards
2. Control plan for plan for tattooist
3. Exposure control plan for tattooist
4. Overview of compliance requirements
5. Disorders and when not to service a client

Professional standards:

1. History of tattooing
2. Business ethics
3. Record keeping: Client consent form, client health history, H.I.P.P.A.A. standards
4. Preparing a station, making appointments, parlor ethics
5. Parlor management: Licensing requirements, Taxes
6. Supplies: Usages, storage, ordering

A FOUR YEAR APPRENTICESHIP REQUIRED CURRICULUM

Hours of instruction of curriculum and performance

- A minimum of an additional 750 hours of curriculum, and 100 successful tattoo performances

  350 hours devoted to the theory and curriculum in the following sections:

Anatomy:

1. Understanding the skin
2. Parts of and the function of the skin

   Tattooing laws and regulations:

   150 hours devoted to the curriculum in the following section:

Sanitation and disinfection:

1. Definition of terms: Sterilization; Disinfection and Disinfectant; sterilizer; Antiseptic; germicide; Decontamination; Sanitation
2. Steam sterilization equipment and techniques
3. Chemical agents: Antiseptic and disinfection
4. Sanitation equipment and procedures
5. Post service sanitation procedures

   250 hours devoted to the practical training in section:

Tattooing:

1. Client consultation

2. Client heath form
3. Client disclosure
4. Client preparation
5. Sanitation and safety precautions
6. Implement of section and use
7. Proper use of and handling of equipment
8. Material selection and use
9. Ink
10. Machine: Construction; Adjustment; Power supply
11. Needles: Configuration, and making of needles
12. Art
13. Portfolio

100 successful tattoo performances:

This guide is a basic structure of the apprenticeship. It is a guide for the Master to keep a structure of instruction and a consistent curriculum. It is a guide for the apprentice to develop as a tattoo artist and gain credibility.

I wrote this guide for the sole purpose of what I expected from my apprenticeship, and how I could make sure my apprentice are completely competent of all aspects of a tattoo parlor. I feel this guide has a sound structure for all Masters to follow.

This industry is booming and as Masters, we need to set higher standards of qualifications as a must. We need to demand more before they walk through the door. If a person seeks employment and has little knowledge of the trade or a small tattoo portfolio, guide the person in the direction of an apprenticeship. I can be confident with this curriculum each and every time the apprentice should have strict criteria to follow.

I was an apprentice under two different Masters. Each Master taught different attributes of our field, first two years were shop structure and basic tattooing procedures. If it wasn't for this opportunity, the other door would have never presented itself. For this I am grateful.

Now my second two year apprenticeship came to me just the same as the first, as if by fate. I was at a real low point in my career and just at that point of uncertainty I was approached by a big red headed dude at the local diner. He acquired about a piece on my neck and gave his compliments to the artist. He left me his card and urged me to call him.

I had nothing to lose, and two days later I made that call and made an appointment to come see him. I was not there in his shop all but twenty minutes when he just burst out with "I might be looking for an apprentice!" and getting approval of acceptance from his wife, I was given another opportunity.

This curriculum sets a clear standard of what each apprentice should be taught. This is an instructional guide for keeping the apprentice on track. This is a review book for those lead artist interested in taking on an apprentice.

I set the professional standard of curriculum for my shop. What do you use for yours? There is so much history about art, not including the amazing tattoo artists that bring the art to life. Let us set our entry level standard for apprenticeship higher and keep this curriculum mandatory, as our own professional standard of all tattoo artist.

Some Masters focus on shop function, others focus on procedures some Masters have sacred trade secrets, no matter the Masters instructional guidance now we all have a professional standard of curriculum. My hope is that all Masters share the same knowledge with each apprentice and pass down to generations to come. I wrote this guide to help me with the knowledge of what I needed to know to guide my apprentice, if this helps you be a better Master and gives your apprentice a better understanding of what is expected. It can turn a long hard road into a nice cool breeze for every apprentice.